In the Year of Leaping Ice

Poems by
Ria Kinzel

BLUE LIGHT PRESS
1st WORLD
PUBLISHING

San Francisco | Fairfield | Delhi

In the Year of Leaping Ice

Ria Kinzel

Cover Art: "Golden Glow at Midnight" by Denise Gallagher.
        With permission.

1ST WORLD LIBRARY
PO Box 2211
Fairfield, Iowa 52556
www.1stworldpublishing.com

BLUE LIGHT PRESS
www.bluelightpress.com
Email: bluelightpress@aol.com

For Eva, Lea, and Miller
With love.

Acknowledgements

With deepest gratitude to Diane Frank for many years of inspiring teaching and encouragement, and for motivating me to publish these poems. They would not have been written without her.

And to all the poets of the Blue Light Press Poetry Workshop, thank you for your support, insightful responses and encouragement.

Thank you also to Joan Kirchhoff for her encouragement and feedback on the South African poems.

Table of Content

Mrs. Archibald

Thursdays after school, my friend Elizabeth
shed "Cheerfulness with Industry,"
"Yes Miss Prout," and uniform green jumpers
to paint blue and crimson swirls,
amber fireworks, oily explosions over stretched canvas
on Mrs. Archibald's tipsy porch,
stroked by fronds of grey-pink bark
that whiskered down the bluegum trees.

Mrs. Archibald wrapped the rocking egg of her belly,
freckled thighs and grubby knees
in skirts that shimmied flowers round her bony ankles
and padded barefoot through sparse dry grass,
aloe flares, poinsettia and red-hot pokers,
dandelions blooming in winter.

From a crook high in the pomegranate tree,
Mrs. Archibald released handfuls of fluffy seed
to cruise the uniform green lawns of weed-killer neighbours –
airy ammunition for guerilla breezes
and the saboteur soil.

I took no lessons with Mrs. Archibald.
She rooted herself
deep in the dandelion cracks of my mind.

Undertones

Apartheid South Africa

There were always undertones –
nannies gossiping with kitchen maids
under the peach trees on lazy Sunday afternoons
while we combed our mango-pit animals.

Men murmuring under blue gum trees
by the humpback bridge
or shouting inquiries into the health of passing strangers.
The hump and rhythm of deep male voices,
synchronizing muscles on the Umfolozi ferry
heaving a boiler up a ramp at Mbabane.

Weaving harmonies of blue-clad maids
offering Christmas benediction in a timbered college hall:
nKosi Sikelel' iAfrica
God bless Africa.

As new laws bit, the tones grew stronger.
Even in the dreariness, even when they shoot us,
we will go –
the rich full voice
of a people's rage, their grief, their hope,
their sustenance, their will.

3

Vuyisile Mini, walking to the gallows
sang
Watch out Verwoerd, the black man is coming!
Watch out Vorster, the black man will get you!
The prisoners joined as he moved through the cell blocks,
clasped him in his people's voice
as he passed.

Toyi toyi
The pulse rises to the beat
running high step
disciplined advance.
Deep throated *Huh! Huh!*
from Zambian bush training camps.
Amandla!
Awethu!

The voice of the people
had not yet reached the white man's ear
when we stalked power lines,
sang tenuous songs in solitary cells
of foreign soldiers and alien flowers
borrowed from Seeger and Baez.
White paper boats
on an unplumbed ocean.

Coming of Rage

When man creates God in his own image
he smells damnation
loses the savor of his labor
curses the act of creation
and grinds the plumed serpent into the dust.

South African Apartheid was rooted in a 17th century
Calvinism, which condemned all things of the flesh
and viewed blacks as sub-human. An early anthem of
the black struggle consisted of variations on "What
have we done? What have we done? Our only sin is
to be black."

1. South Africa

At daybreak, Sarel Celliers, astride a gun carriage, vowed:
"Almighty God, we swear to Thee a Holy Covenant.
Smite down the might of the Zulu nation
and we will honour Thee this day forever.

God answered the need of his chosen people
and they honored their Covenant,
hallowed this day each year to affirm:
If you, God, will subject the black race to our yoke
we will honour you."

What have we done? What have we done?

Sgt. Bart Coetsee of the South African Police
burns an inconvenient black body out in the veld.
He trades jokes and beer with his partner,
barbecues steaks on a smaller fire.
Comingled smoke of roasting flesh ascends to the sky.

Black detainees jump to death from high windows,
break their jaws tripping on concrete floors,
go home in sealed coffins.

The Reverend Danie Viljoen
and his black maid stand trial for sexual intercourse.
He found innocent, she guilty.
Black men hang in unremarked succession
for the rape of white women.
It is black women who bear coloured babies.

Four out of five babies born at Baragwanath,
Johannesburg's vast black hospital,
die of poverty before the age of two.

What have we done? What have we done?
Our only sin is to be black.

2. Childhood

I am baptised in Blood River water,
cherished in a silver chalice.

On a distant farm
our nursemaid's toddler tumbles into the cooking fire
while his grandmother nods.
The hospital crams him three to a bed – to die.
My mother brings him home,
daily changes stinking bandages.
His shrieks pierce marrow.
Daily I run till the screaming stops.
He lives to dance. I may not play with him.

Grandmother speaks: "If you run through the house,
God will send you to Hell to burn forever."
What if I spill my milk – or sing in the bath?

What have we done? What have we done?
Our only sin is to be born.

My sister, curious at the age of eight,
watches a chicken lay an egg.
Grandmother washes her mouth with carbolic.
God speaks: Be fruitful and multiply.
Grandmother speaks: Filth!

Nightmare whispers: I dance in gay procession
with flowers, music song.
I am the bride. At the altar
a black beetle awaits.

I look in disbelief at the wet red blood
that soaks my white winter panties.
I'll have to tell.

My mother, seeing her last innocent babe
sink into womanhood
laughs hysterically and long.
I stand in the bathroom door,
wait for the laughter to stop.

What have I done?

Mother speaks: Change regularly so there's no smell.
No one will know.
What if they do?
What if they smell the sweet blood smell?
Will they laugh at my presumption?
I feel so presumptuous,
but at night, crouched over homework
a sense of secret power
seeps sweet through my veins.

Dream warns:
Peacefully, I sit by my grave in my straw high school hat,
handful by handful throw soil on my coffin
bury myself deep in dark earth.

My mother sends home our nubile maid.
Ntombi smiles, happy to visit her mother.
She bears a sealed letter instructing the farmer
to beat her with a horse whip
for seeing a man at night.

What have we done? What have we done?
Our only sin is to be woman.

3. Young Woman

A visiting policeman boasts to my pretty sister:
After the riots when we found wounded kaffers,
we shot them in the head.

Cousin Maggie peed in the same potty,
shared dolls and stolen cookies.
Now she crosses silky legs, strokes her snowy petticoat,
and speaks: "I change twice a day – then I know I'm clean."
I read such a sad story in the *Woman's Weekly*
about a girl who stays home every night
hoping a man will come.
She reminded me of us.

The voice of the poet:
"Stand up, stand up for Jesus."
It's a little late for that.
Stand up for justice and a jolly life.

At Sharpeville, police gun down
113 black men, women and children
in the back, running.

What have we done?
What have we not done?

The crones speak: All men are beasts,
but you young girls, you must get married.

Dream forebodes:
Draped in musty lace curtains, I walk down the aisle
compelled by the massed will of veiled women
towards an uncouth youth
who waits at the altar.

Maggie speaks: "I will get married – to someone –
anyone – the postman…"

My sister sits sullen, says nothing.

Daniel scrawls on his lecture notes:
"Have you heard of Che?"

Mandela speaks from the dock:
"The time comes in the life of any nation
when there remain two choices –
submit or fight.
We shall not submit."

Beneath my bed, a trunk heavy with dynamite.
Detonators on the shelf above
spark a haunting sense of secret power.
Maggie perches on the edge of the bed,
sandwiched between explosives.

Goodbye dear cousin, sister, mother.
I will no longer cling to cold cement,
waiting invitation to an alien dance.
I won't play victim to the sins of my fathers
while the floodwaters rise.
Forget Perseus.
I'll take my chance on the sea beast.

For petty theft, a nearby farmer
rams a hose down a boy's throat, turns on the tap.
Accidental death, sentence suspended.

For those things we have not done
that we ought to have,
Lord, forgive us.

Bride

Before dawn on a wintery morning,
I, and others who come by different roads,
pull on black ski masks,
blast the signal cables on all suburban routes.
The trains glide to a halt.
Cape Town shuts down.

4. Epilogue

Thirty years later, Mandela walks free,
births a rainbow nation.

My high school teems with Zulu girls.
The staid cathedral swings with black harmonies.
Mini businesses on mats crowd city sidewalks
with used clothes, carvings, love potions.

I am robbed by a Xhosa at gunpoint
in the photocopy shop.
Poverty growls.
Wealth retreats behind razor wire.
White men join black to sleep under bridges.

Dawn light casts long shadows,
but when I walk down city streets,
black eyes meet mine as equal.
Tokoziele and I grin, high five,
compare crop pants in a dress shop mirror.
I feel at home in my country.

The Guest Book

South Africa, 1964, solitary confinement

Twilight sifts through fanlight bars –
the landscape is familiar here.
High cragged walls of grey close in,
reach up to tangled winter boughs.
Naked pipes twist over the ceiling sky,
and underneath me as I lie,
a rough veld pad of matted undergrowth.

The solitude is comforting,
liberating.
No one who loves me can intrude in here.
No one can steal my consequences.
The eye at the spyhole is indifferent.

On the walls, graffiti
like trunk-carved hearts in lovers' woods.
Marie loves Fransie,
and someone recommends the Song of Solomon.
On the door frame
Stephanie has scraped her days:
Very bad
Okay

Depressed
Afraid.
Lyn, only her date of arrival.

I don't take up the crooked nail.
One does not sign the guest book at home.
This present caging holds no fears –
only the prospect of a life unlived
howls the mind to splinters.

Seesaw

My sister,
being of sound mind,
refused the task of firstborn –
becoming scapegoat.
It fell to me
to become the family lightning rod,
the grounder.

I made over all expendable parts:
intellect to dome-browed father and tooled leather books,
relationship to a wounded Pieta,
power to a swollen-bellied mantis,
cracking the earth with eggs.

I stuffed myself full with familial imaginings –
solitary confinement of the soul,
reduced myself to a sharp seething point
that popped the enchanted bubble
and balanced saint with sinner.

If my sister had chosen the other way,
would I, playing sinner, have sought to be saint
and she, being saint, have sought flame?

And what would have been the difference?

In the Year of Leaping Ice

Far North, Canada

The whirlpool below the rapids churns relentlessly,
tears off ice chunks eight feet thick.
In serene dignity, icebergs circle sateen swells,
mirror the procession of stars
that spark through waves of gossamer.
The earth swings beneath our feet,
slung about by swiftly increasing daylight.

Most years, the ice rots uniformly,
flows out in silent pans.
This spring, the river mouth won't budge,
digs in, defends its slow-won territory.
Near its source in the cracked granite,
swells of the Shield, the ice decays, careen downstream
overpower the whirlpool
bear down, pile up, shove and push,
compact with sudden shifting force,
sharp cracks of cannon fire
that rocket ice blocks skyward.

It slices the settlement in two,
shoots down the slender power line,
blasts air strip and deep-drilled water holes.
The midwife frets on the bank.

Overnight, the ice-jam breaks.
The river tosses free.
The midwife hauls out her canoe
and Minnie Philipoosie, bearing down,
expels her squalling son.

Memory of Direction

Emerald Lake, British Columbia

The moose that left deep tracks across the lake has gone.
The snow field stretches smooth and white to the distant
shore,
where age-striated mountains slash the sky.
Pillows of snow caught by the sun
sparkle like diamonds on their black-firred reaches.
Distant crack and rumble of an avalanche.

Under the ice, dormant trout, fins winter-stilled,
retain faint memories of fly-snap, splash and ripple,
glimpses of reedy banks, whispering the busyness
of small scurrying life –
field mice, crickets and butterflies
among columbine, saxifrage and buttercup.
A hundred shining rivulets gush from grey crags,
trip along fault lines, embracing perpendiculars,
giggle across stones.

Milky glacier-melt reflects the sky as emerald
swells the lake, stirs deep currents
urges resumption of slow, sure movement to the sea.

Sisyphus

I stumble groggy down the stairs to pick up
the morning news that thumped on the doormat.

In the cool early light,
a fresh tuffet of snow slides
down a fingertip of fir,
dints the quiet surface of a thick-packed chalet roof.

A wolverine
black, sleek, sinuous
peers over the roof ridge,
rears tall,
observes the stillness of the lake,
the quiet trees.

He drops flat on his muscled belly
and swooshes down to the eaves,
spins,
bounds undulating
to the high-pitched crest,
spins slides
spins leaps
fanning wild lacy arcs of snow
in ceaseless ecstasy.

A More Fitting Gift

That evening when you returned,
your face was open, vulnerable as a dove-gray moth
emerging from its silk cocoon –
as on the day the priest joined our hands together.
My gift of a newly covered chair seemed unworthy,
even crass.

I wanted to tell you I had missed you
and about Molly's new tooth.
You wanted to talk of Linda,
the generosity of her smile,
the way her green dress shimmered
like sunlit birch leaves in a spring breeze
around her slenderness.
Your parting kiss.

So I listened,
sitting beside you on the back steps.
Our yellow daffodils burned gold,
ignited by the scent of lilacs
beyond the fence.

Grace Notes

1.
The first time I kissed him
in the late-night kitchen,
coffee steaming towards perk
his face opened like a wildflower to sunrise
sixty years ago.

2.
On her wedding day, my distant sister
forgoes rivalry,
takes my hand and walks me down the gilded hallway,
as she did when I was three.

3.
Between Sesame Street and walking the terrier,
we get down to business:
Pee in the pottie, Matt! Pee in the pot!
Rush to the fridge door, search, search, pounce!
Drop the magnetic 'P' in the pot.
Mutiny cedes to pure glee.

4.

Laughter brimming over, he runs to me:
Come see! Come see!
Lipstick zigs and swirls over sink, mirror and walls.
That is not funny! Not one bit funny!
He retreats, considers, returns.
Not funny for you. Funny for me!

5.

Great Grandma, on a warm October day
inches her walker down the sidewalk.
Grandma keeps pace beside her,
knees high.

6.

Annie, after long absence,
hides behind a kitchen chair,
emerges inch by inch,
dances a solemn jig of welcome
on stubby, chubby legs.

7.

Saying goodbye under Grandma's jacaranda,

Matthew firmly retreats from lip-puckering neighbour
aunties,

reaches up to kiss Tokoziele,

who bakes spicy drumsticks and sweet creamy custard,

draws flag-tailed warthogs on band-aids.

Flagrant defiance of taboo.

She backs off fearful. The missus nods approval.

They hug long and hard.

8.

Arrogant adolescent

slouched against his locker door.

Ben has me impaled on a pin,

until the comedy of my impotence

stirs laughter in my eyes.

Oh..? Oh..? He disappears.

Tonight, the computer will not eat his homework.

9.

I teach meditation to a corn-rowed Zulu girl –
shabby classroom in a riot-scarred school.
The door crypt-creaks in the gusting wind.
A fight breaks out by the window – curses, stones fly.
Did the noise bother you?
Please, Tembi whispers, may I do it at home?
It's so quiet inside me.

10.

Family camping in the Alberta Badlands,
my aging knees balk at high-cut stone steps.
Matt grasps my hand, hauls me up.
Our eyes meet.
We smile at the role-reversal.

Recipe for an Angel

Take one *Reader's Digest*,
fold the pages diagonally,
fan to form free standing cone, paint white.
Add styrofoam ball for head,
gold giftbox string for hair.
Punch circles of felt for eyes and mouth.
Gold pipe-cleaner halo, size of a silver dollar.
Glue on paper doily wings.
Attach pipe cleaner hands, holding song sheets.

In the foyer, Room 12's angels
flock on a sheet of crimson satin.
Gold halos rise over golden hair,
white robes immaculate, filigree wings.
Little hands hold tiny hymnals
with miniature words in gold.
Blue eyes raised skyward, their blush-pink mouths
sing sweetly in perfect unison
around a shining star.

Room 13's angels, uninvited
boogie across a Tigger tablecloth at the back of the gym,
do nothing in unison.
    T-Rex angel gives a deep-throated roar.
        White knight angel takes his lance to war.
    Ginger-cat angel hugs a blue mouse.
        Pitbull angel has a beagle for a spouse.
Winged Princess Leia and R2D2
        teach C3PO to chop, Kung Fu.
Cat-in-the-Hat angel.
        Black leather bat angel.
Green angel, rose angel,
        finger-up-her-nose angel.
            Devil, scarlet devil
                with a halo for a tail.

When the lights go out, one snowy angel,
halo slightly askew,
hitches a ride on an errant draft
and joins the riotous crew.

Orchestration

Grade 5

Today, we will focus on writing instructions:
Be precise, to the point, use imperative voice.
Write clear directions for painting your face.
No talking – we have laryngitis.
Now paint your partner's face.
We have panda faces, dragon faces, scarred goalie masks.
Ninjas, blue Batman, Yoda with green ears.
She made me a zombie! I described a princess!

Green slime in a pie plate.
Viscous planet in Betelgeuse, named Goop,
solidifies under pressure:
Design a spacecraft to land on it.
Sarah's ship, flat and heavy, hardens its own landing pad.
Joey's circling lasers toast the surface to a deck.
Haley's ship skims the surface, scoops like a duck.
Mary, if you flick it, you wash the wall at recess!

Why is Lisa lurking behind a binder screen?
reading Tolkien – leave her be.
Has John-o got his squeeze-ball to help contain his hands?
Granola bar for Fran. No breakfast in that house.
Jennie's mom got drunk again.

Rapt silence around the author's chair.

Witch Wars VII holds us spellbound.

More coming, says Teri, with an alligator grin.

Piston-fisted Curtis writes of taming the Beast Man.

Tam's poem of a wet pink mouse whispers her abuse.

Twenty-nine workbooks *Open at page sixty-eight*.

If it's boring, fake it! The test – we've got to make it!

Devil take it!

City Sidewalk

The sun rests easy in the hammock of an elm,
the pavement tanned by snowmelt.
Rooted on the library steps, a bag woman,
blousy as a rain-drummed peony, shouts:
Where you striding, white hair lady? Chill!

Nubile girls gather like flocks of flamingos –
smooth, shapely legs, brown, cinnamon, pale
weave and blend.
Hipster dudes preen. Their barbelled biceps and torsos
blossom butterflies, skulls, flaming snapdragons.
Small boys rejoice at a purple turd
etched on a muscled calf.

Nurtured by the returning sun, patio bars have sprouted.
Girls, energized by pizza and iPhone
flaunt hair, hug, twitter.
Brooks Brothers bankers, open-collared, metro-sexual,
savour tankards of boutique beer.
Lovers preen and coo.

The red-haired youth at a corner stall
slathers ketchup, green pickles and mustard.
A daycare files by. Small hands clutch a rope vine
that sprouts bubblegum ice cream cones.

The woman on the library steps raises unkempt hands,
smiles wide at the proffered hotdog:
Bless you lady! Bless the sun!

Writer's Block

On Mongolia's high plateau
chill winds pierce flesh with needle teeth.
A spellbound traveller watches a wrinkled monk
leap, twist, whirl his cudgel, howl
beat back thin air.

Unceasingly, he battles his demon,
six twisted horns and a scorpion tale, says the abbot.
Someday he will know it's a figment of mind
and stop.

The traveller sets down this marvel among others
in his leather-bound journal.

My mind rattles its fetters,
cudgels the debris of caustic cousins, acidic elders,
Miss One-Right-Answer Prism and old Snake-Tongue
Grimes.
Children must answer — not question.
Girls conceive babies, not books.
The rusty chains clatter, jerked upside and which way,
cats-in-a-trashcan racket.

I must set down this wonder in a poem,
scraped by my fingernail in soot.

Tonsure

Response to Warning Poem by Jenny Joseph

Not a red hat
so gallantly defiant – so strenuous.
No big blossomy brims requiring a smiley face.
Nor baseball cap loyalties, logos or maxims
tiresomely defining.

A cloth hat, I think, rain dimpled, brim floppy,
mottled and mellowed like old tarnished copper.
A hat to be at ease in, like a green frog on a sunny lily pad,
to carry blueberries, swat wasps, and water thirsty terriers.
It will serve to cover the bald spot
until I think I can bare it.

Hopscotch

There was a time when I aspired
to individuate elegantly, with dignity.
I hopscotched marble tiles in the college library
in silver sandals with a rose between my teeth,
perched defiant miniskirts on tottering stilettos.
I had no interest in scruffy blue jeans,
weed, or pill-permitted promiscuity.
I aimed to liberate black Africa
in a black cashmere ski mask.

Sixty years later,
no longer hopping
sure-footed as a mountain goat,
I did bum-slides down the basement stairs today,
my bandaged foot flapping like a storm-tossed peony,
to sit bobbing on a rebounder
to the swell of Handel's Hallelujah!
Just another eccentric old woman
redeeming indignity
with laughter.

A Matter of Self-Respect

Thumping rock.
Tessellated steel struts, cages and beams,
iron wheels, pulleys, cables,
weight and counterweight.
Angled metal fractals in counterpoised mirrors
acres of tangled steel –
driven by sweat and aspiration.
Body builders sculpt
bulge biceps, pump pecs, twitch glutes
harden hamstrings, ripple abs.
Barbell champs.

Runners drop
jump squats, split squats, pistol squats.
One-legged knee raises, one-legged hops,
bird dogs, clam shells, burpees, squats.

Climbers strain
push ups, pull ups, dead hangs, frog,
shoulder dislocaters, barbell squats.

Downsizers plank
hardstyle, weighted, three-point planks.
Kick box, punch bag, battle rope, row.

What is your goal? her trainer asked,
splendidly sculpted in Spandex.
Will you climb mountains? Or run a marathon?
All she wants
is to hand back her wrinkled body at the final gate
in working order,
spine somewhat erect.

On Clearwater Bridge

Astride the current,
Clearwater Bridge provides firm footing,
a rail to rest crossed arms above the stream.
Sunlight dabbled ducks,
trout spray-flash, pearl dragonfly,
flash stab of heron's beak.
A kayaker's lazy J's, a peacock paddle.
A child waves from a passing car.
Canary school bus slows dark hearse,
twilight flick of a skewbald mane.

Now taillights secure the dark
unless fire, flood or deep earth tremors
rattle the footbed, shake foundations,
immerse in turbulence
and send us grasping for a higher span –
steel girders, earthworks, straws.
Perhaps instead, from earth to sky,
a sinuous steel-spun thread.

Caduceus

In Apostolic churches, sanctified bread becomes
the body of Christ. It is kept in the altar to main-
tain His Presence at all times except at Easter.

On Good Friday, she finds bare cloth,
the altar stripped, the Presence gone.
Desolate, she knows
long years as a priest-tease are ending.
She's not much for crucifixes, catechisms, even the Confiteor,
but this oneness of body and Being
vivid in absence
she can pledge faith to.

At confirmation, the altar decked, something shifts.
Heart on hold, her body weeps.
Her mind hopes she will not drip on the bishop,
who dubs her knight in Christ.

At lunch a priest inquires: How does it feel?
From the deep storage cellar of her mind the answer seeps:
It's much like losing one's virginity.

Consternation of clerical brow!
But she remembers the morning after
striding the tundra, exultant in new-found womanhood.
This time, she's claimed a fuller humanity
and feels . . . less apologetic.
Just that: a little less apologetic.

In a long-distant struggle,
learning to tamp dynamite,
she recognized the same dark joy
in deep and secret power
as on the night the moon exacted its first blood tribute.

Sensible of the priesthood, she thinks
to be leery of the serpent presence.

And Mary Spoke

After a Gnostic Gospel text

Jesus having departed to the temple,
the disciples sat disconsolate
in the shade of an olive tree.
"Who does He mean?
Those that have ears, let them hear?"
asked Thomas.

But Peter, the impetuous,
demanded of Mary,
"Tell us what it was like to conceive Christ."

It is forbidden! It would burn you to a crisp!

But the twelve urged her,
hunger in their eyes,
yearning in their calloused fingers.
Mary pitied them and spoke
and they knew
God's fingertips brush Adam's,
clay takes on life,
the blinding light of a tiny child, pure spirit.

Flames shot from Mary's mouth
their robes burst into flame
the stars fell, mountains shook,
great tides swept the earth.

Then Jesus took her by the hand,
whispered, "Peace, be still."

Pieta

1.
Once she was ravenous
whipped, caged, furious,
a leopard who slashed her children's viscera
sucked marrow from the bones of their stories.

Now, tended by a kind maid, a remote husband,
she sits on a sunny veranda – arthritic and alone.
Cold in her Canadian down coat
and New Zealand sheepskin slippers,
she gums her loneliness, regret, bewilderment,
fumbles and refolds with pain-clawed hands
scant bundles of cautious letters.
"Sharper than a serpent's tooth is an ungrateful child,"
as King Lear knew.

2.
She does not know that the rueful eyes
of her far-flung children,
seeing the godly cruelty ricochet
across scarred generations.
At times of thanksgiving their tongues speak

of swirly home-sewn dresses, rich fruitcake, river picnics.
Only their hearts cower like naked virgins
behind fear-frosted glass.

3.
She does not know that the house shadows
whispered in different
voices.
At her, the whiskery matriarchs hissed:
"Thou shalt not!"
"Fear Hell. Fear God. Fear life."
"Jesus may not save you."

Her mother's voice pierced the eldest daughter:
"Sick. Wicked. What you touch you destroy.
Give your son to your sister. She'll save him
from you."

The youngest heard her mother croon:
"Disposable. Make your life mine.
I will drive your chariot, flee the four grim horsemen
evade the flames."

4.

She does not know that when news of her death comes,
her daughters will unite in hysterical laughter,
over the long-distance phone,
releasing tenderness,
trickling rivulets of glacier melt in May

for the loving child strapped
the frightened girl crushed
the passionate nurse denied
the lonely wife distanced
the wounded mother yearning

for all mothers yearning for lost children
who fear their mothers' love.

She does not know
they can now begin to forgive
themselves.

Metamorphoses

Sunset edges crimson clouds with gold
smudges to mauve, gray, dim
vanishing in night's cool embrace.

Raindrops darken earth's red dust,
seep into soil and thirsty roots,
transform to life's green sap.

The harsh cries of *hah-de-dahs* echo,
linger across a thousand aloe-flamed crags,
unfold the vast geometry of Africa.

Rocked by the train, my mind teems.
Words melt, sentences fall apart,
mesh continents and generations into patterns,
webs of spider tracery
till thread by thread life makes sense
and fear gives way to love.

At 17,000 Feet

Scattered white clouds define a denser world below,
dusty and warm,
the linear geometry of road and field disrupted
by unruly, ox-bowed rivers.

The muddy-booted farmer
sees cloddy fields, striped and stubbled,
feels rain, shade, sun.

I soar unmoving in cool, clear light –
the steadfast course of outshone stars
unseen above.

A Kind of Absolution

I feel their quiet presence
in the rustling silence of green parks,
the stillness of near sleep,
the half light of the morning kitchen.

A gentle flock
like blue-gray doves fluffed soft in the early cool –
the dead do not leave us.

Freed from the bondage of eyes, ears, fumbling fingers,
they must now know
the children I've betrayed,
the friends neglected,
the spits of malice, armor-plated lies,
the secret strutting rooster.

And yet, like neighbors gathering under porchlight
to mark the wayward backpacker's return,
they seem to love me.

The emerging moon makes known gnarled stands of
trees.

Questions of Voice

1. In the beginning

There was a time when I knew I had no voice
and it didn't bother me.
Ideas and obedience spoke in my father's voice –
glow lamps along a narrow corridor.
Feeling and obligation, anemone tentacles,
spoke in my mother's.

There were times I said "I want,"
but that was selfish.

Sometimes, I checked to see if I was really there:
I am not my body, my feelings, my mind –
stripped down to a still, small point
of such infinite significance
that everything was all right.

2. Brass bands and panpipes

One is supposed to have a voice.
English teachers tell you so, and revolutionaries.
Silence creates unease.
Why so quiet? Speak up!

People did:
Repent or burn. Jesus saves. God is dead.
When we found an injured kaffer,
we shot him in the head.
Honour your father and mother.
Stand up for justice and a jolly life.
All men are beasts – young girls must marry.
They lived happily ever after.
Love rejoices in the truth,
bears all things, endures all things.
Heil Hitler.

Brass bands and panpipes, bagpipes and flutes
blasted the daytime, clapped hands over ears.
At night, when echoes faded
and *I want* battered *I am*,
hellfire filled the void.

3. Smelting

If voices become too numerous to identify,
like ingredients in a back-stove stew pot,
does that mishmash become your voice?

And what if under great stress that voice fragments
like splinters of smashed glass:
the speaking voice - naive librarian,
the censored radical voice
the trivial voice – *that one would be cute out of uniform*
the calculating voice: *that worked, not this*
the smug voice of approval: *you're good at this*
the ironic voice: *regular Tower of Babel*
the absent voices of fear and rage
held at bay by the voice of decision
playing the stops
the observer, noting.

If these sounds then transform to light,
globules of color, like pressured coal to diamond,
flowing as a stately river into the mouth of significance,
and if you flow with it
into the peace that passes understanding
and return with a new voice,
is that your voice?
Or simply an alloy of cheap base metals
smelted in the fire.

4. Who speaks?

I have spent my life learning to read and write,
to distinguish your voice from mine.

Neurons change hands in a fluid country dance.
Old patterns melt, weave new tapestries,
cruel battles, tender trysts, gazelles.

When I tell my son he is beautiful,
is that his voice, or mine, or ours?
If I love the wrong person
and hear myself whisper, *I'm ugly, stupid bitch*
whose voice is that?
If I modulate my voice so you can understand me,
is that your voice or mine?

5. And now?

In the years of getting and begetting,
voices earn t-bones, bagels, borscht,
boutique B & Bs in Paris.
They cry, *Oh, yes!* Snarl, *Keep off!*
Vow I do! Announce, *You're fired!*
They map the roads that others took,
identify the buds of May,
the lusty green of a sunlit slope,
the slough of dull despair.
Chart starry orbits,
Unified Field and Superstring
Tao – Baha'i – God, Three-in-One –
lacy tessellations
to corral space and time.
We build fences for our safety,
destroy them by our growing.

Can I still afford a voice.
now that my hands are age-spotted and tremble?
Might I not, sinking into the grave,
score deep grooves in coffin walls
with clawed fingers, clutch for
stripped neurons, DNA, voice
to blot out the looming void?

Shouldn't I now prepare to merge
Voiceless,
a raindrop slipping quiet into a clear still pool
into the fullness of that silence
into which voices dissolve
and from which they return.

Glossary and Notes

Undertones

nKosi Sikekel' iAfrica	Hymn that became freedom song, then National Anthem.
Vuyisile Mini	Union and protest organizer, songwriter.
Verwoerd	Prime Minister.
Vorster	Minister of Justice.
Toyi! Toyi!!	Highly energized, running step used in protest marches.
Amandla! Awetu!	Power! To us!

Coming of Rage

Sarel Celliers	Preacher, before the Battle of Blood River, December 16, 1838.
Zulu	A major South African tribe.
Veld	Grasslands.
Baragawanath	Johannesburg's black hospital; largest hospital in Africa.
Blood River	Where white guns defeated Zulu spears, 1838.
Carbolic	Harsh Laundry soap.
Kaffers	Heathens, blacks.
The voice of the poet	D.H. Lawrence
For those things….	Anglican Book of Common Prayer.
Xhosa	A major South African tribe.

About the Author

Ria Kinzel grew up in South Africa. After clashing violently with the Apartheid government, she emigrated to Canada to teach Inuit students in the Far North. In a complete u-turn, much of her time since then has been devoted to fostering world peace. She has taught elementary and high school English in Alberta and Iowa. Central to her pedagogical theory is the prevention of boredom through high interest and student initiative. Her interest in meditation led to the study of India's Vedic literature. She currently lives in Calgary, close to family and the Rocky Mountains, where she teaches meditation and leads poetry workshops.

Printed in the USA
CPSIA information can be obtained
at www.ICGtesting.com
JSHW022336151223
53849JS00001B/105